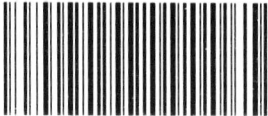

GW01402622

FUTURE FILES

EMERGENCY PLANET EARTH

A BEGINNER'S GUIDE TO SURVIVAL IN THE FUTURE

MIKE
FLYNN

COPPER BEECH BOOKS
BROOKFIELD, CONNECTICUT

© Aladdin Books Ltd 1998

Designed and produced by
Aladdin Books Ltd
28 Percy Street
London W1P 0LD

*First published in the United States
in 1998 by*
Copper Beech Books,
an imprint of
The Millbrook Press
2 Old New Milford Road
Brookfield, Connecticut 06804

Editor
Simon Beecroft

Design
David West
Children's Book Design

Designer
Malcolm Smythe

Picture Research
Brooks Krikler Research

Illustrators
Ross Watton, Stephen Sweet (Simon Girling
Associates), Richard Rockwood, Alex Pang

Printed in Belgium
ISBN 0-7613-0823-7 (lib. bdg.)
ISBN 0-7613-0742-7 (trade)

A CIP data entry for this book
can be found at the Library of Congress.

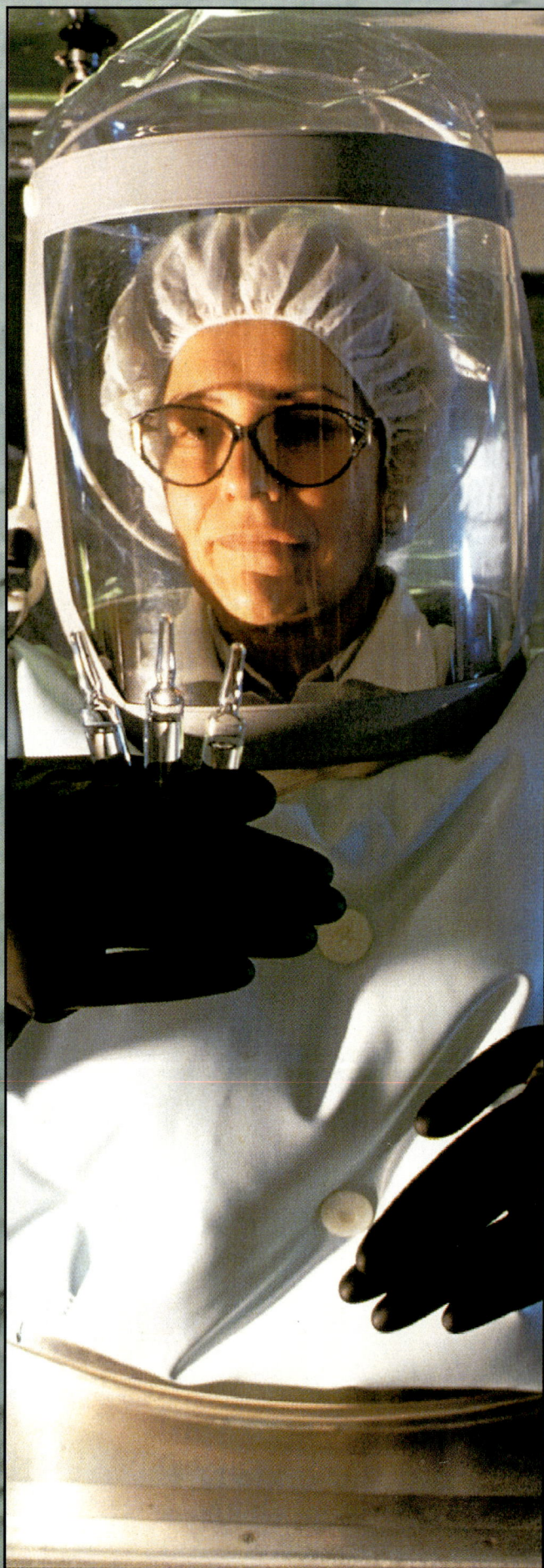

MISSION CONTROL

INTRODUCTION

The earth has led a charmed life. Over the last four and a half billion years, it has not only managed to avoid total destruction, but has produced the conditions under which life can flourish. As far as we know, no other planet in our solar system can boast as much as a single living life-form.

But at times in its past, the earth has come close to destruction. Scientists believe that the dinosaurs, who dominated our planet from 220 to 65 million years ago, were wiped out when a large meteorite crash-landed: They have found a huge impact crater off the coast of Mexico. New evidence suggests that the fate met by the dinosaurs was not unique. The Bronze Age civilizations of Egypt, Mesopotamia, and Greece may have been destroyed by showers of giant meteors.

In 1994, the planet Jupiter crossed the path of a large comet (*see* pages 8-9). If the earth had crossed the comet's path instead, almost all life on the planet would have been destroyed. This event focused attention on the importance of monitoring potential threats to our planet. Human beings are skilled in the art of survival. As our technology advances, we will discover new ways to protect our species — even if we have to spread out across the galaxy and beyond.

This book looks at the range of potential threats to our planet, including new forms of killer diseases (*see* pages 20-21), future ice ages (*see* pages 22-23), even black holes (*see* pages 10-11), and asks: What can we do to ensure our survival in the coming centuries?

Right *Need to tell science fact from science fiction? Take a look at our Reality Check boxes. We can't see into the future, but these clever devices tell you how realistic an idea is. The more green lights, the better. The "how soon?" line guesses when in the future the idea might become reality: Each green light is 50 years (so in the example here, it's 100 years in the future).*

REALITY CHECK

FEASIBLE TECHNOLOGY	●	●	●	●	●
SCIENCE IS SOUND	●	●	●	●	●
AFFORDABLE	●	●	●	●	●
HOW SOON?	●	●	●	●	●

THE RESTLESS EARTH

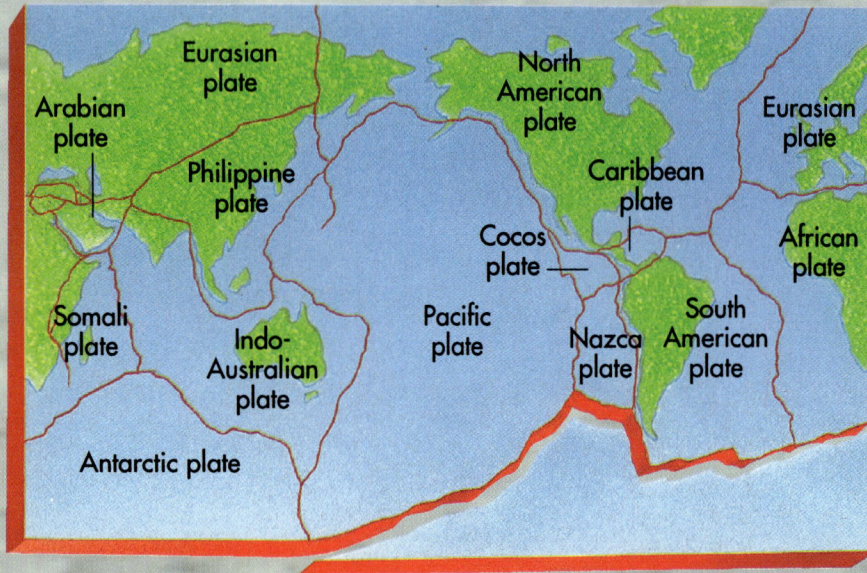

Map labels: Eurasian plate, Arabian plate, Philippine plate, North American plate, Eurasian plate, Caribbean plate, Cocos plate, African plate, Somali plate, Indo-Australian plate, Pacific plate, Nazca plate, South American plate, Antarctic plate

Left *Over the next 50 million years, the map of the world will change as continents move and break up, and new islands form. North and South America may become separate continents. As the continents change, new forms of animal will evolve, while others will become extinct.*

SATELLITE MONITORING

Scientists are now looking into ways to improve our warning capabilities for volcanoes and earthquakes. Increasingly, highly sensitive satellites are used to monitor minute movements in the rocks below the earth's surface. The next stage will be the Global Seismographic Network (GSN), in which satellites will be integrated with a permanent network of 128 recording stations positioned uniformly over the earth's surface.

Scientists predict that the next century will witness more volcanoes and earthquakes than ever before. These violent activities are produced naturally by movements of the earth's surface — but human activities, such as mining, may be causing more.

FIERY FUTURE

The earth's surface is broken up into pieces, called tectonic plates. Earthquakes and volcanic eruptions are caused by movements of these plates. It is thought that oil and gas, deep within the earth, form natural "shock absorbers" between the plates. By removing oil and gas, we may be bringing about the destruction of our own cities in the 21st century.

Right *Prediction may never be an exact science. Future scientists may focus on improving defenses against earthquakes. For example, "smart" building materials will be able to absorb shocks.*

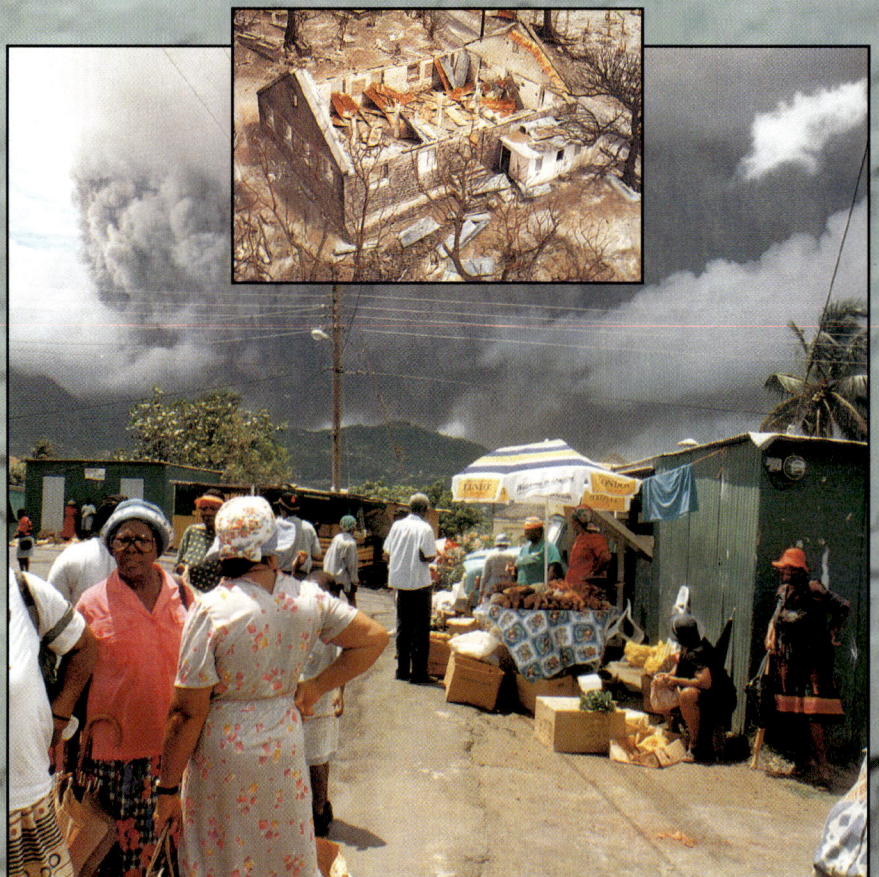

WATCHING THE CLOUDS

NASA's Earth Observing System (EOS), a series of remote-sensing satellites launched in 1998, will monitor volcanic activity. In particular, it will track eruption clouds, which can affect the world's weather.

PREDICTING EARTHQUAKES

FEASIBLE TECHNOLOGY	🟠	🟠	🟠	🟠	🟠
SCIENCE IS SOUND	🟢	🟢	🟢	🟠	🟠
AFFORDABLE	🟢	🟢	🟢	🟢	🟢
HOW SOON?	🟢	🟢	🟢	🟢	🟢

FIRE FROM THE SKY

The earth is constantly threatened by rocks from space, most significantly asteroids and comets. Until recently, we would have had little or no warning before impact. But new systematic surveys using next-generation technology will significantly improve our capabilities to detect near-Earth objects.

DEEP IMPACT

In any one year, there is a probability of roughly one in 100,000 of the earth being hit by an object from space. An asteroid with a diameter of one mile would hit with more destructive force than all of the bombs dropped this century. It would cause a global earthquake that would wipe out cities worldwide. Massive waves would rush inland, causing devastation for thousands of miles. Huge amounts of dust would be thrown up into the atmosphere, blocking out the sun and causing the death of nearly all life on this planet.

Left *In 1994, fragments of a huge comet called Shoemaker-Levy 9 collided with the planet Jupiter. Huge holes up to twice as wide as the earth were punched in its atmosphere.*

SPACE WATCH

The best way to avoid a surprise encounter is to be aware of potential threats. This would give us time to find ways to divert the oncoming object (*see* page 9). Discoveries of very faint or distant objects are increasing due to the introduction of telescopes equipped with technologically advanced cameras called charge-coupled devices (CCDs). These cameras have light detectors made of silicon, which is 100 times more effective than the most sensitive photographic film. One such project is NASA's Near-Earth Asteroid Tracking (NEAT) system, set up in 1995. By 2020, it aims to have a complete check of all space rocks that may come near the earth in the future.

Below *Comet Hale-Bopp appeared in the skies in 1997 and was studied by astronomers worldwide. In 1998, a probe will travel billions of miles to explore a comet called Wild-2. It is due to return in February 2006.*

Below *Meteor Crater was made when a meteorite struck 40,000 years ago. In the next century, an asteroid called 1997XF11 will make several passes close to the earth.*

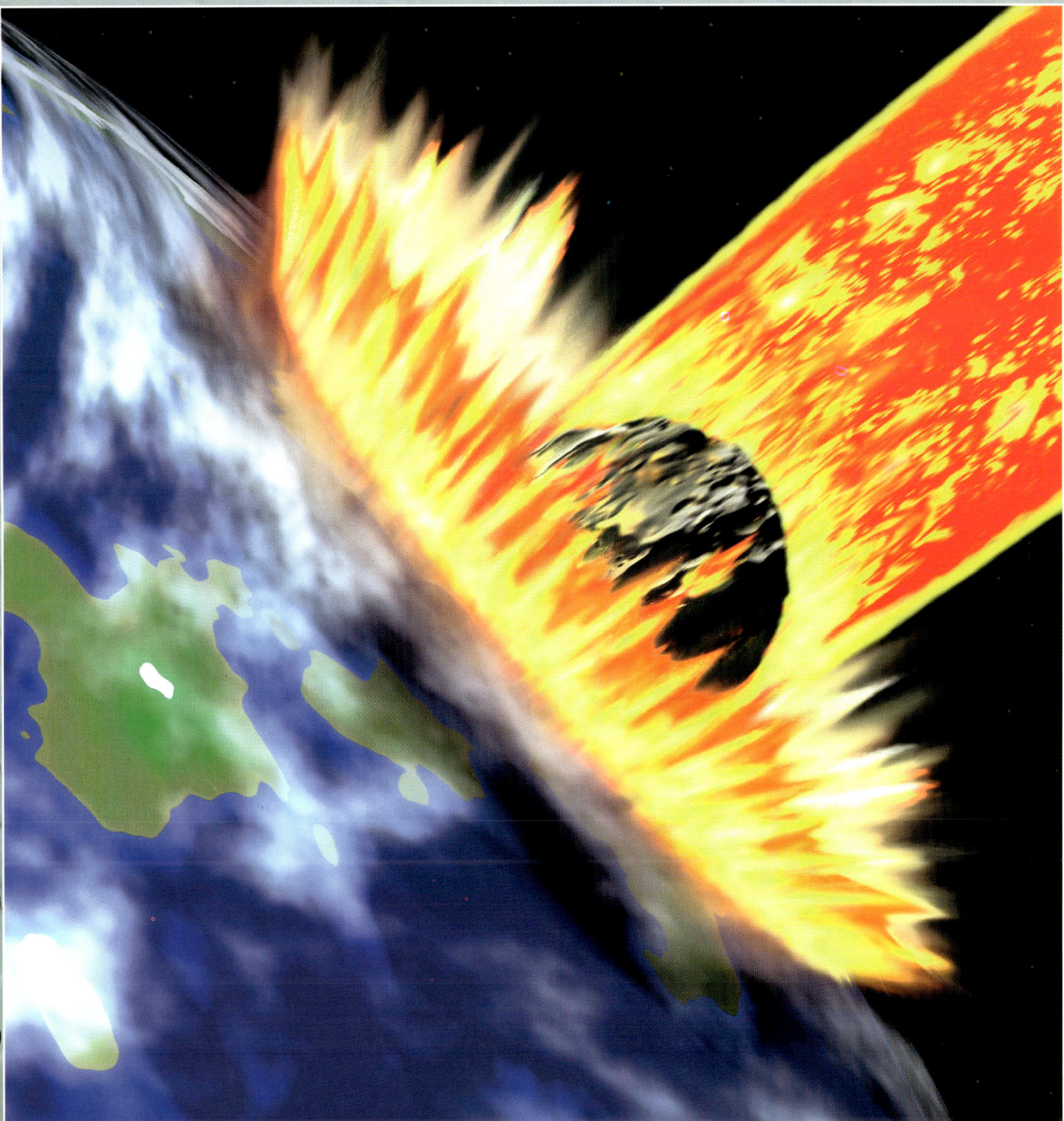

SHOT DOWN

NASA's Space Guard Survey looks at ways to avoid collisions with asteroids or comets. One suggestion is to position powerful missiles in orbit around the earth to blow up an oncoming middle-sized space rock before it reaches us. An alternative proposal is to use remote-controlled space rockets to nudge it away.

METEOR SMASHER

FEASIBLE TECHNOLOGY	🟢	🟢	🟢	🟠	🟠
SCIENCE IS SOUND	🟢	🟢	🟢	🟢	🟢
AFFORDABLE	🟢	🟢	🟠	🟠	🟠
HOW SOON?	🟢	🟠	🟠	🟠	🟠

BLACK HOLES

No object in the universe is more dangerous than a black hole. These massively dense objects cannot be seen — their gravity is so strong that nothing, not even light, can escape. Anything that gets caught in the gravity of a black hole disappears forever.

INVISIBLE THREAT

Black holes are invisible to ordinary telescopes. Instead, radio telescopes and satellites are used to pick up invisible X rays given off by objects falling into one. There are two kinds of black hole: smaller ones that orbit a star, and huge ones that lurk in the center of galaxies (huge groups of stars). There is a black hole at the center of our own galaxy. In 1997, scientists measured it and found it to be 2.5 million times heavier than our Sun. Evidence has also been found for four smaller black holes in our galaxy, two of which are spinning at more than 10,000 revolutions per second, dragging nearby objects around with them.

COSMIC TRASH CANS

But black holes could be used to our advantage, too. If garbage was dumped in from a safe distance, it would disappear completely from our universe.

Above *Cygnus X-1 is thought to be a black hole in the constellation Cygnus.*

CERTAIN DEATH

Neutron stars — from which black holes form (*see* page 11) — are sometimes mistaken for black holes. They are also dangerous. If one neutron star collides with another, the resulting "gamma-ray burster" creates enough destructive energy to wipe out any civilization within 1,500 light-years. The next gamma-ray burster in range of the earth is expected to explode in 300 million years – with devestating consequences.

Right *Our planet orbits a star (the sun), which is just one star among millions in a spiral-shaped galaxy called the Milky Way. It is thought that spiral galaxies are turned by super-massive spinning black holes in the middle. The brightness at the center of the galaxy is caused by millions of stars that are turning around the black hole.*

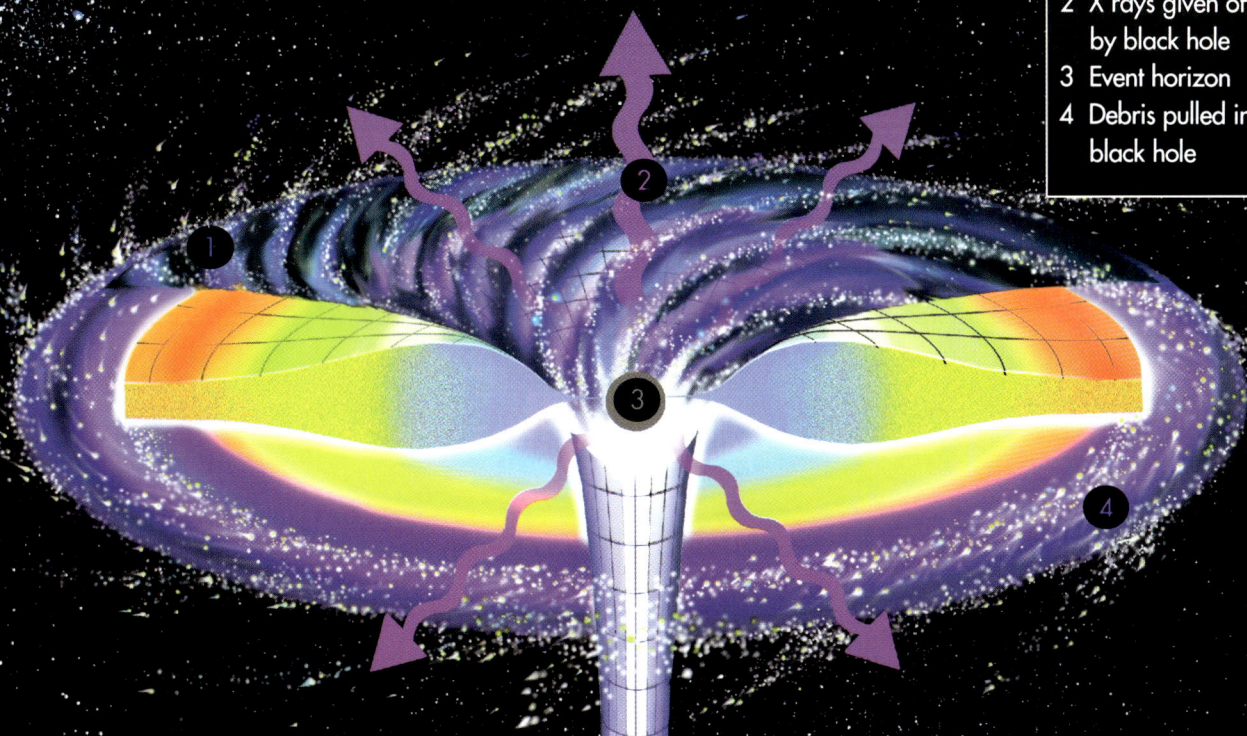

EVENT HORIZON

The boundary of a black hole, the point just past which there is no escape, is called the event horizon. The force of gravity is so great at the event horizon that an object weighing just 2 pounds on Earth would weigh 1,000 billion tons.

ROVING BLACK HOLES

ADVANCE WARNING?	🟢	🟠	🟠	🟠	🟠
SCIENCE IS SOUND	🟢	🟢	🟢	🟢	🟠
ESCAPABLE?	🟠	🟠	🟠	🟠	🟠
HOW SOON?	🟢	🟢	🟢	🟢	🟢

FORMATION OF A BLACK HOLE

Stars cluster together in galaxies (1) and can be different sizes. Black holes are formed from very large stars (2), with a mass about 30 times that of our Sun. When these stars die, they do so in a huge explosion called a supernova (3). All that is left behind is the very dense core — called a neutron star — that keeps on collapsing back in on itself, until it disappears into a tiny, but massively dense, point — a black hole (4).

ARE WE ALONE?

If aliens were ever to visit the earth and make their presence known to us, life for everyone on this planet would change forever. Over the last few decades, the search for extraterrestrial intelligence has intensified, with a number of projects scanning the skies for signs of life.

Left and below The current interest in UFOs was sparked by a reported UFO crash at Roswell, New Mexico, in 1947. An alien was rumored to have been found.

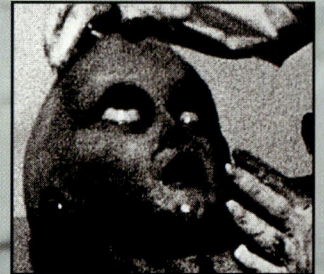

LOOK TO THE SKY

The best way to search for signs of life in the universe is by using radio telescopes. Assuming intelligent life could have invented radio, these telescopes listen for any unusual radio signals coming from space. In 1993, NASA set up a project called the Search for Extraterrestrial Intelligence (SETI), with a budget of $10 million a year. SETI focused on nearby stars, but after a year of operating, had found nothing and was closed down. Since then, private organizations have continued the search. Project Phoenix, based in California and Australia, searches both the northern and the southern skies.

UNEXPLAINED SIGNALS

Another project, carried out by Harvard University, has picked up a number of possible artificial signals from space. However, none were repeated, which suggests they were not deliberate, since any alien wanting to make contact would repeat a message over and over until it had been heard.

SETI projects are expected eventually to move to the far side of the moon. A radio telescope sited here would not be disturbed by signals from Earth. Japan intends to build a remote-controlled radio telescope there by 2009.

ALIEN DESIGN

There is no reason to assume that an alien would look like us. We have arrived at our current shape after millions of years of evolution, during which many changes occurred that would not necessarily happen elsewhere. However, if life has evolved by a similar process on other planets, there are advantages to be gained by having limbs, eyes, gas-breathing lungs, and a sense of smell — however they are arranged!

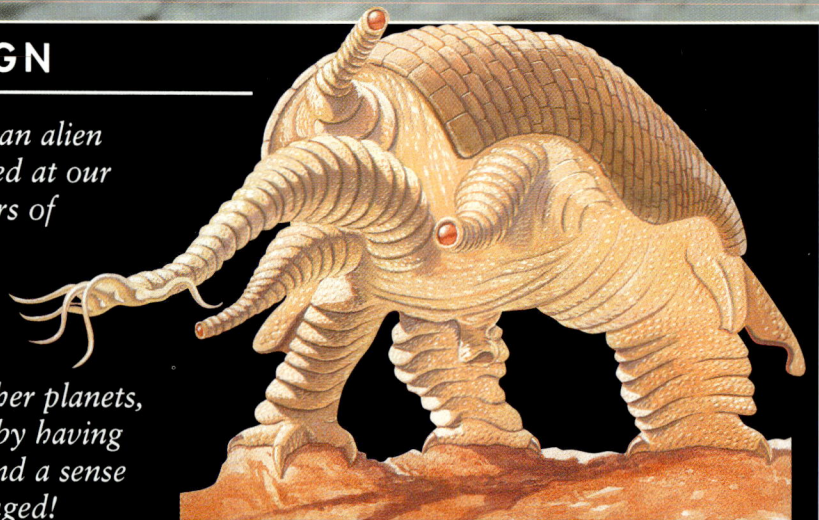

MAKING CONTACT

FEASIBLE TECHNOLOGY	●	●	●	●	●
SCIENCE IS SOUND	●	●	●	●	●
AFFORDABLE	●	●	●	●	●
HOW SOON?	●	●	●	●	●

IS THERE ANYONE THERE?

The Very Large Array (VLA), in New Mexico, is a group of radio telescopes used to search for alien life. But contact with aliens could prove to be fatal for human life, as movies like Independence Day *(1996, main picture) have imagined.*

FRIEND OR FOE?

Travel over the vast distances of space requires highly advanced technology. Any creature capable of reaching us is bound to have technology that is far superior to our own.

WHY TRAVEL?

Aliens would need to have a good reason for traveling to Earth. The nearest star to us that is thought to have planets in orbit around it is at least six light-years away. This means that, even traveling at the speed of light — 186,420 miles per second — it would take six years to get here. Because it isn't actually possible for any creature to travel at the speed of light, it would take them much longer. And this is just to consider the nearest star to us. An important question needs to be asked: What would they want from us?

Left Aliens may come in peace, as in the movie Men in Black *(1997). They could even live among us, creating a truly multicultural society!*

SPACE PIRATES

The earth possesses several natural resources that are not to be found anywhere else in our solar system. Chief among these is an abundant supply of liquid water. As water is so rare in our own solar system, it might be safe to assume that it would be rare elsewhere. Perhaps our alien visitors will be space pirates, trying to plunder the scarce natural resources of the galaxy and possessing a technology that we would be powerless to resist. Or they may simply be space travelers looking to explore strange new worlds. For all our sakes, let's hope they are.

Above It may be unrealistic to expect all aliens to be friendly. This one, in the movie Alien 3 *(1992), certainly isn't.*

Above The aliens in Mars Attacks! *(1996) are comical but deadly — an unlikely combination in real life.*

Above The alien in the Predator *movies hunts down "lesser" species (humans) and kills them for fun.*

TECHNO ALIENS

Machines are far better suited to life in space than delicate flesh-and-blood creatures such as ourselves. It is possible that in our first contact with extraterrestrials we may actually meet machines — perhaps microscopic robots far in advance of the tiny machines made so far by our scientists (below).

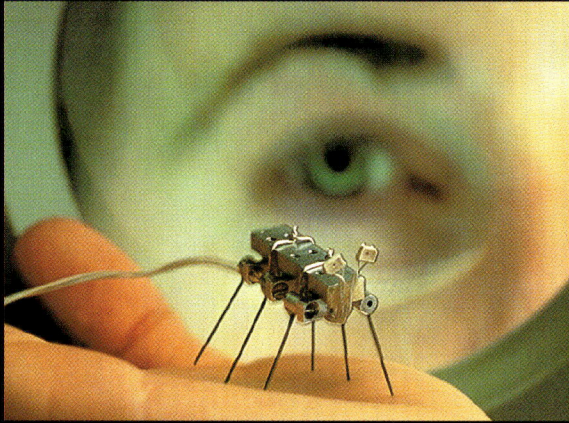

ALIEN LIFE-FORMS

FRIENDLY?	🟢	🟢	🟢	🟠	🟠
MORE ADVANCED THAN US?	🟢	🟢	🟢	🟢	🟢
HUMANOID?	🟠	🟠	🟠	🟠	🟠
HOW MANY?	🟢	🟠	🟠	🟠	🟠

FUTURE WAR

Above *The futuristic city depicted in the movie* Robocop (1987) *is so dangerous that robots have replaced human police.*

The threat posed by asteroids, comets, and black holes, is small compared with human potential for destruction. With nuclear weapons, we already have the power to wipe ourselves out. We will probably continue to put new technologies to destructive uses.

ANTIMATTER

A highly deadly weapon would be antimatter bombs. Antimatter is a strange form of destructive energy: It occurs naturally only in rare circumstances, such as when stars collide. Scientists have created tiny amounts of it in laboratories. Antimatter bombs would be so destructive that they could only be used for warfare in space.

GRAVITY BOMBS

Another lethal weapon could also be the simplest: dropping metal onto a target, such as an enemy military base, from a great height. Known as gravity bombs, they would use an electronic guidance system to release a heavy metal object from just above the earth's atmosphere. Gravity would then accelerate the object to such a high speed that it would land on a target with the force of an asteroid (*see* pages 8-9). The target would be entirely destroyed, leaving no trace of what caused the destruction.

Right *This soldier uses a heat-seeking camera built into his helmet to track an enemy. Could this be the soldier of the 21st century?*

Above *Movies like* Terminator (1984) *imagine a future where robot warriors can rebuild themselves if they are shot.*

NONLETHAL WEAPONS

But not all weapons need be lethal. So-called nonlethal weapons are currently being developed. They include a glue gun that literally sticks the enemy to the spot without causing lasting harm.

ROBO WARRIORS

In the distant future, wars may be fought by cyborgs — part human, part machine. Wearing night-vision range finders and heat-detecting goggles, they would be fitted with powerful artificial limbs. Using technologies only now being developed, they may rely on information gathered by remotely controlled robots, and could use trained dogs to detect enemy soldiers and mines.

GRAVITY BOMBS

FEASIBLE TECHNOLOGY	🟢	🟢	🟢	🟢	🟠
SCIENCE IS SOUND	🟢	🟢	🟢	🟢	🟢
AFFORDABLE	🟢	🟢	🟢	🟠	🟠
HOW SOON?	🟢	🟠	🟠	🟠	🟠

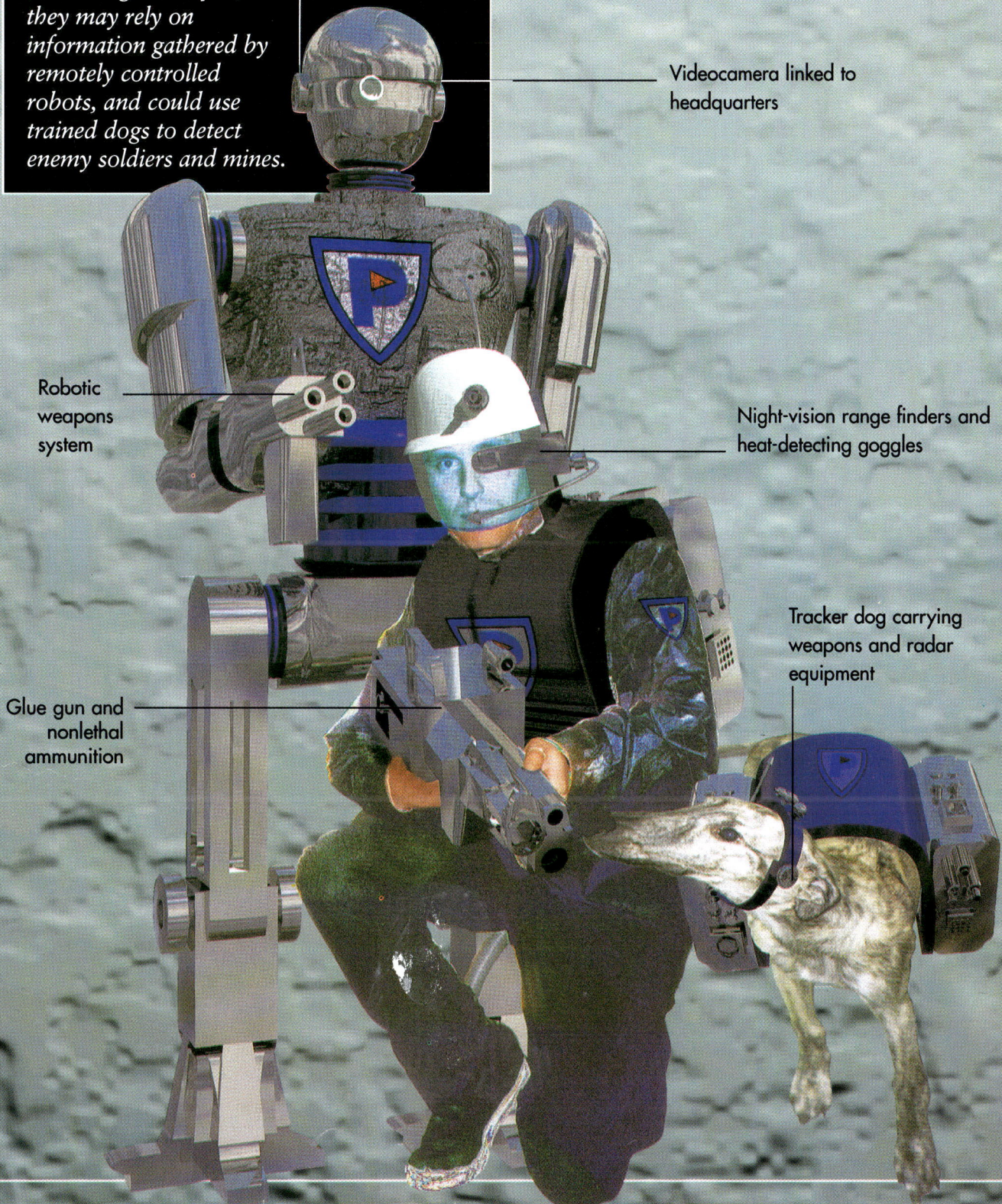

Videocamera linked to headquarters

Robotic weapons system

Night-vision range finders and heat-detecting goggles

Glue gun and nonlethal ammunition

Tracker dog carrying weapons and radar equipment

17

DISEASES FROM SPACE

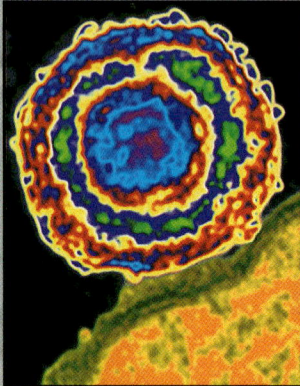

Above *This common virus is just 50 millionths of an inch across. It is shown emerging from the surface of a human cell.*

No one is sure how life began on Earth. One theory is that it arrived from space. New evidence for this theory was provided by the appearance of Comet Hale-Bopp in 1997. In this comet astronomers found traces of chemicals that make up living organisms. Now, some scientists think that viruses may also have arrived from space — and that more may be on the way.

HOW A VIRUS TAKES HOLD

Viruses are tiny organisms that invade the cells of living things. They cause diseases such as measles, influenza, and the common cold. Viruses use the cells' reproductive systems to make copies of themselves before spreading out to infect other cells. If we are healthy, we can fight off viruses by producing molecules called interferons, produced by the infected cells.

Below *In 1984, a meteorite that had come from Mars was found in the Arctic. Inside were tubelike structures that appeared to be fossilized bacteria, a primitive form of life.*

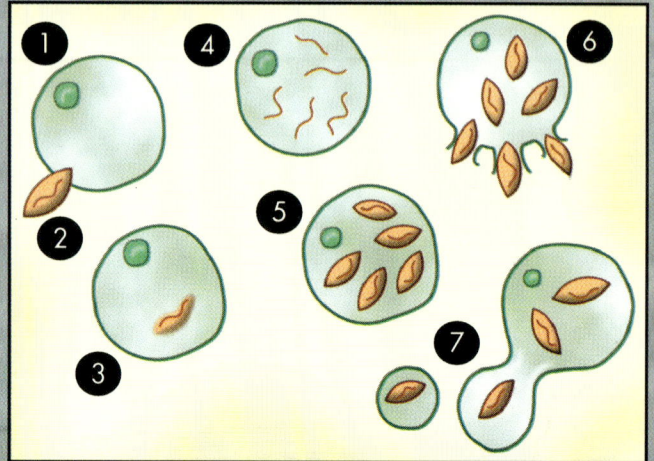

Above *After a healthy cell (1) is invaded by a virus (2), the virus sheds its shell (3) and starts to reproduce itself (4) inside the cell. As the virus multiplies (5), it destroys the cell and begins to spread (6) to other cells. Some of the reproduced versions of the virus even take a part of the original healthy cell with them (7) to feed on as they look for a new cell to invade.*

SURVIVING IN SPACE

Over the last few decades, astronomers have established that microscopic organisms, such as bacteria and viruses, can survive in space. Evidence for this was discovered as early as 1969, when astronauts landed on the moon. Among other things, they recovered a camera from an earlier, unmanned spacecraft. When scientists did tests on it back on Earth, they were amazed to discover bacteria, which has been accidently carried from Earth, still alive on it.

NEW SCIENCE

This has led to speculation that bacteria and viruses are introduced into the world from space. If this is so, then diseases of which we have no present knowledge could also arrive in the future — causing a widespread outbreak. The study of evidence for traces of life in space has become a new science, called astrobiology (*see* page 19).

FIGHTING VIRUSES

FEASIBLE TECHNOLOGY	🟢	🟢	🟢	🟠	🟠
SCIENCE IS SOUND	🟢	🟢	🟢	🟢	🟠
AFFORDABLE	🟢	🟢	🟢	🟠	🟠
HOW SOON?	🟢	🟠	🟠	🟠	🟠

BUGS IN SPACE

In April 1998, NASA set up its first astrobiology institute, to study the evidence for how life might arise in the universe. Over the course of the next century, this organization will investigate more closely comets, as well as other planets and moons, hoping to find further evidence of alien bacteria and other microscopic organisms.

SUPERBUGS · Unstoppable menaces?

In the first half of the 20th century, medicine made great advances against diseases caused by bacteria. Antibiotics played a large role in destroying, or at least reducing the severity of, many diseases. But as the century closes, some bacteria are evolving strains that can survive current antibiotics. "Superbugs" could become a deadly menace in the 21st century.

ANTIBUG DRUGS

When antibiotics are used against bacteria, they destroy most of them, but not all. Some resist the effects of the drug and are able to use the antibiotic next time to become stronger. These super-resistant bugs could become unstoppable. A recent study found that, under the right conditions, three entire continents — Africa, Asia, and Europe — could become infected with a deadly superbug within two weeks. If this bug were to mutate (change form), that process may take only days, or even hours.

FIGHTING BACK

The ability to fight superbugs using new antibiotics or by modifying existing ones is proving less effective. The newest approach is to fight the bugs from the inside — by altering the genetic structure of the bacteria themselves.

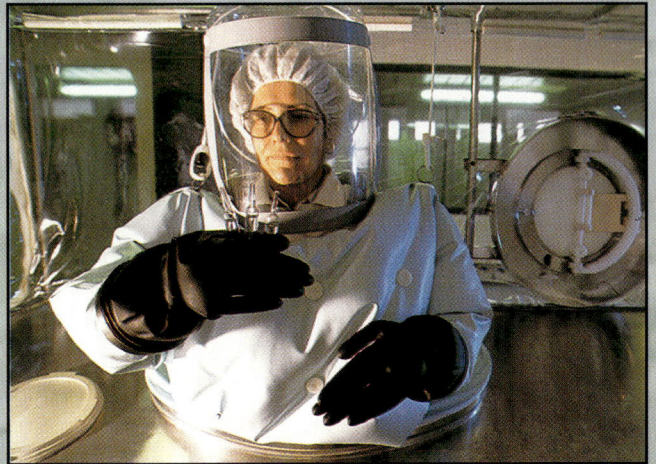

Above *Some of the world's most lethal diseases are stored in high-security research laboratories. Scientists here attempt to find ways to fight new strains of deadly bacteria.*

CHANGING GENES

All living things, including bacteria, are controlled by chemicals inside them called genes. Researchers at Yale University are developing ways to stop the genes that make the bacteria resistant to specific antibiotics from working. Early in the next century, this method will be tested on humans. If successful, it could bring today's most useful antibiotics up to strength again.

Left *With larger numbers of people moving around the world, scientists fear that superbugs will spread, too. However, the real 21st-century killer could be the hamburger. In the future, it will be ever more common for fast food to be made in one place and then sent around the world, an infected batch could affect thousands of people.*

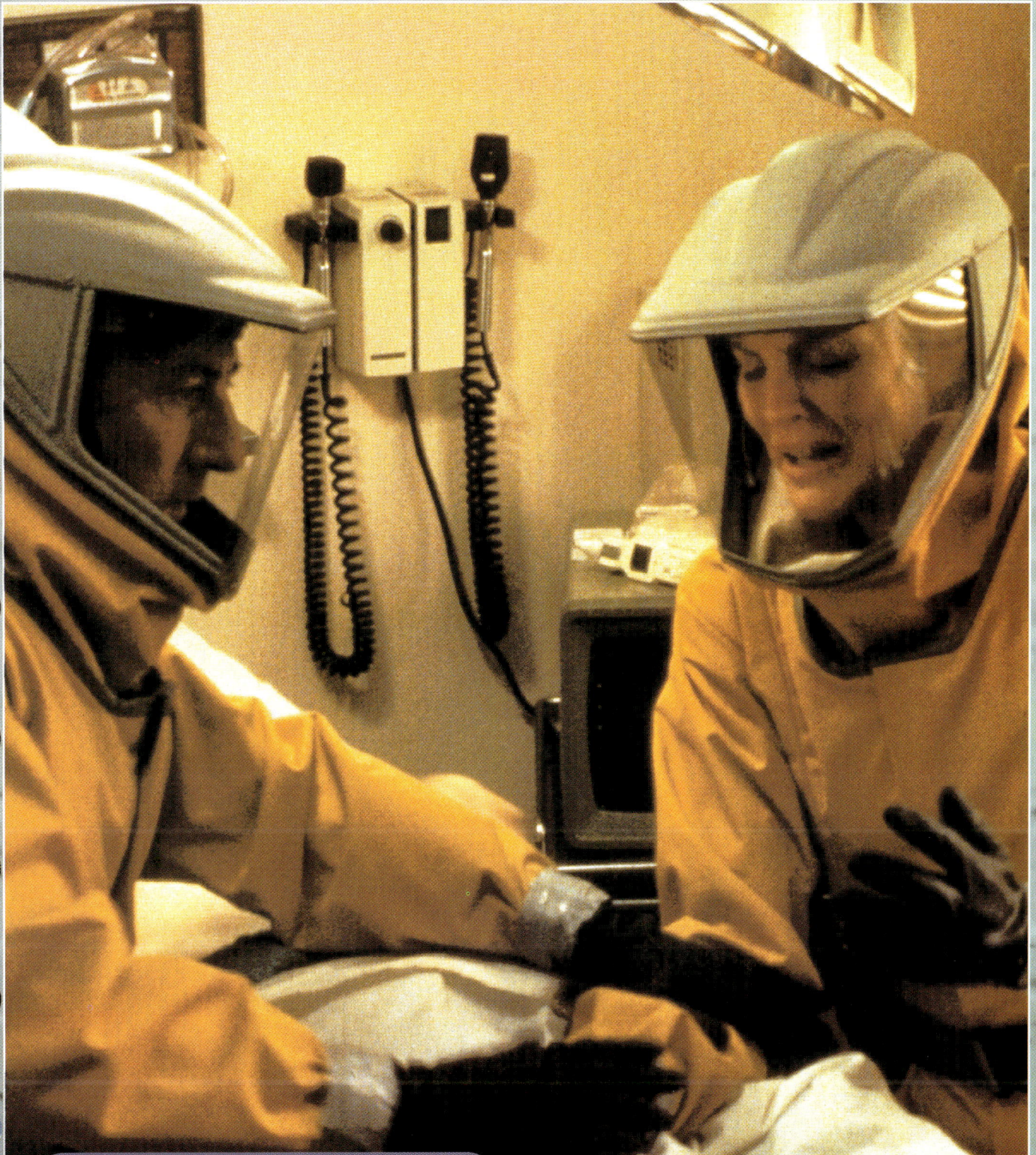

FIGHTING SUPERBUGS

FEASIBLE TECHNOLOGY	🟢	🟠	🟠	🟠	🟠
SCIENCE IS SOUND	🟢	🟢	🟢	🟢	🟠
AFFORDABLE	🟢	🟢	🟢	🟠	🟠
HOW SOON?	🟢	🟠	🟠	🟠	🟠

OUTBREAK

In the movie Outbreak (1995), a dangerous germ escapes from a laboratory. It attacks and kills in hours. Although there has been no recent outbreak like this in the world, the possibility of its happening in the 21st century worries experts.

THE NEXT ICE AGE

For perhaps half of the earth's history, and certainly long before human beings roamed the planet, there have been ice ages — periods when ice sheets covered large regions of land, creating a climate of strong winds and continual snows. The next ice age is already overdue, so scientists must come up with a way to halt it.

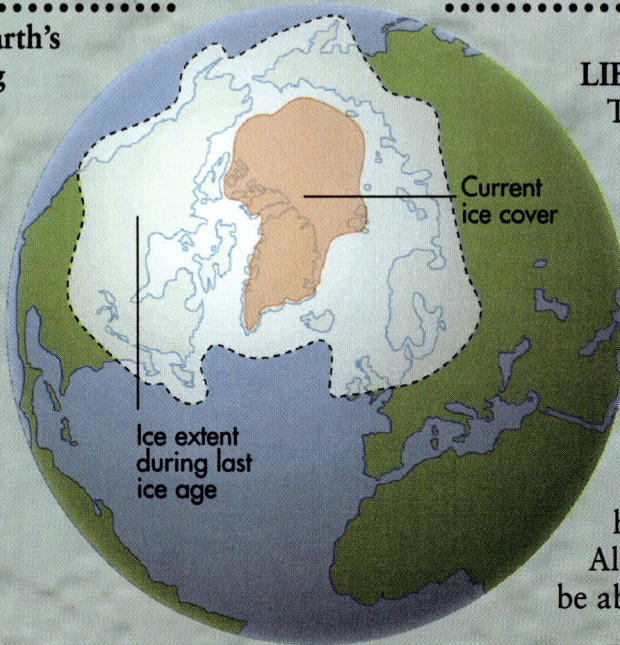

Current ice cover

Ice extent during last ice age

THE BIG FREEZE

Previous ice ages each lasted from 20 million to 50 million years. As little as 10 percent of the last two million years have been periods like our own, with a warm climate. Many factors combine together to cause ice ages. One of the most important is long-term changes in the earth's orbit around the sun. Over thousands of years, the distance at which we travel around the sun can alter by millions of miles, affecting the climate.

Above *The most recent ice age, which began about 3.5 million years ago, advanced south from the North Pole to cover Canada, Greenland, Siberia, Scandinavia, and most of Britain, including the North Sea.*

LIFE IN THE FRIDGE

The next ice age will completely change the way future generations will live. As the ice spreads, cities like the ones today will no longer exist. Millions of people will try to move to warmer areas nearer the equator, causing huge overcrowding. Alternatively, we may be able to adapt to the frozen conditions by building houses from ice — as native people of the Arctic, such as the Inuit, do today.

RAYS OF HOPE

Some ambitious thinkers believe the next ice age could actually be prevented from happening altogether. If giant mirrors were placed in orbit, extra sunlight could be reflected onto the earth, keeping the temperatures up and holding back the ice.

Right *Antarctica is a frozen continent around the South Pole. In a new ice age, ice sheets will advance from the polar regions (here and at the North Pole), destroying billions of homes. Based on evidence from previous ones, scientists think that when an ice age begins, it can effect the climate all around the world in just 20 or so years.*

FROZEN CITIES

The last time the Arctic expanded southward, it spread across the North American continent and reached as far south as the area just below the Great Lakes. If this were to happen again, cities such as New York would be virtually wiped away by gigantic, slow-moving sheets of ice, called glaciers.

SURVIVING AN ICE AGE

FEASIBLE TECHNOLOGY	🟢	🟢	🟢	🟢	🟢
SCIENCE IS SOUND	🟢	🟢	🟢	🟢	🟢
AFFORDABLE	🟢	🟢	🟢	🟢	🟠
HOW SOON?	🟢	🟢	🟢	🟢	🟢

GLOBAL WARMING

The earth's average temperature has increased more in the last 100 years than at any other time in the last 10,000 years. If it continues at the same rate, global warming could be disasterous for life on Earth in the 21st century, causing droughts, spreading deserts, and — due to melting ice — floods.

Above If global warming continues, ocean levels could rise by 28 inches by the end of the 21st century. This will cause serious flooding in many low-lying countries, such as Bangladesh.

CLEAN ENERGY

Global warming is caused by adding to "greenhouse" gases in the atmosphere, which trap some of the heat from sunlight. Chief among these gases is carbon dioxide, produced by fossil-fuel power plants and car engines. One future solution could be nuclear-fusion power plants. Unlike today's nuclear power, which is produced by fission (smashing apart atoms), nuclear fusion forces atoms together. This creates energy but no radioactive waste. U.S. scientists aim to have a commercial fusion plant working in the early 21st century.

GETTING RID OF GAS

Another proposed solution involves freezing carbon dioxide from the air and storing it in space. Much simpler, though, would be adding iron to the oceans. This has recently been shown to increase the amount of plankton (microscopic organisms) in the water, which suck large quantities of carbon dioxide from the air.

Left and right One solution to overdependence on cars, particularly in cities, will be the introduction of Zero Emission Vehicles (ZEVs). Currently being tested, ZEVs will be powered either by advanced batteries or by hydrogen fuel cells, which create electricity by a "clean" chemical reaction.

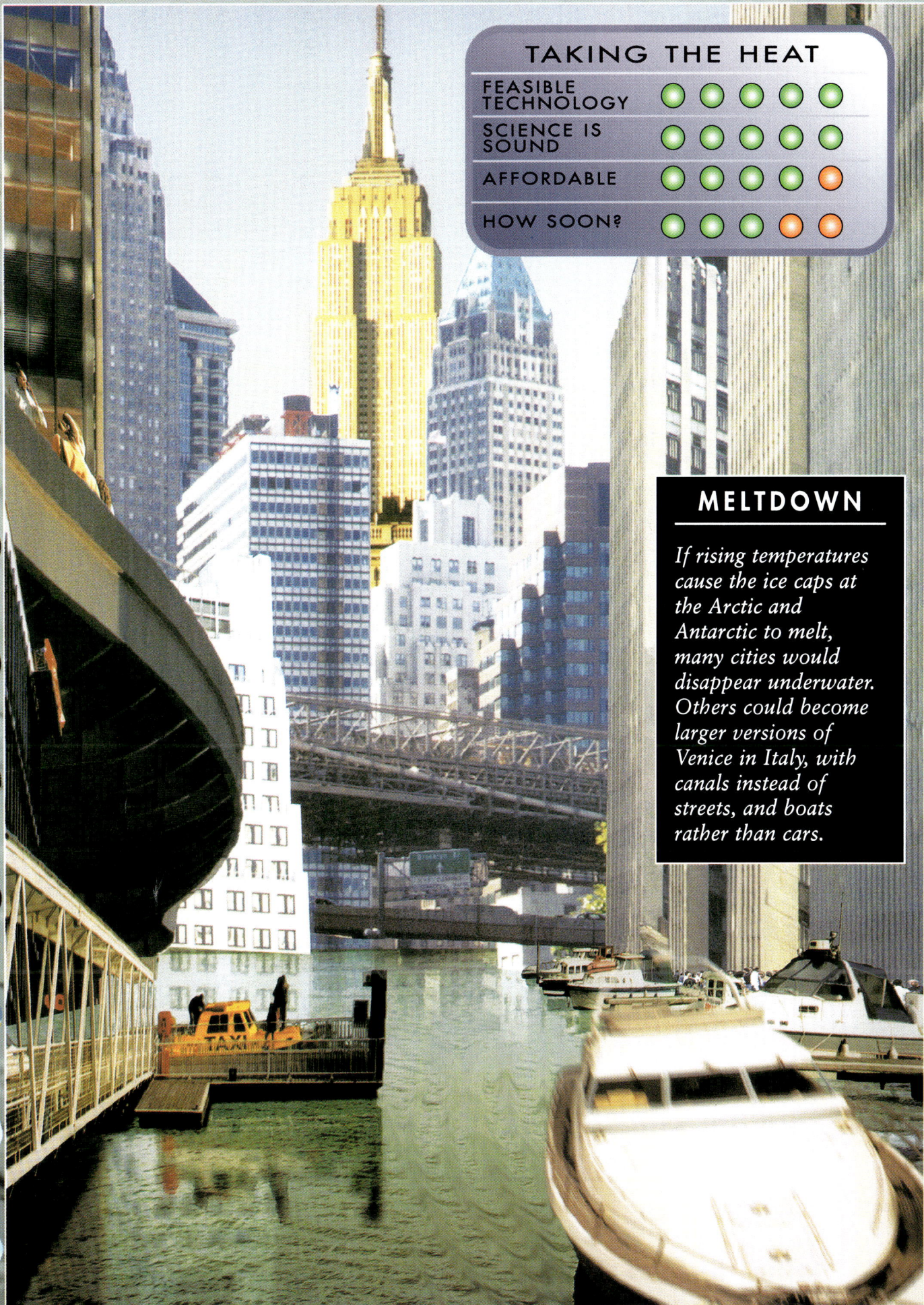

TAKING THE HEAT

FEASIBLE TECHNOLOGY	🟢	🟢	🟢	🟢	🟢
SCIENCE IS SOUND	🟢	🟢	🟢	🟢	🟢
AFFORDABLE	🟢	🟢	🟢	🟢	🟠
HOW SOON?	🟢	🟢	🟢	🟠	🟠

MELTDOWN

If rising temperatures cause the ice caps at the Arctic and Antarctic to melt, many cities would disappear underwater. Others could become larger versions of Venice in Italy, with canals instead of streets, and boats rather than cars.

SUNBURST ·

The end of our Sun

The sun will eventually die, taking all traces of life on this planet with it. But don't worry about it just yet. It isn't due to happen for another five billion years.

NUCLEAR POWER

The sun's heat is produced by nuclear reactions inside it — producing the equivalent of millions of nuclear bombs going off every second. In five billion years, the sun's fuel — hydrogen — will begin to run out. When this happens, the sun will begin to swell, changing in color from yellow to a deep red. Then, over another 100,000 years, the sun's diameter will grow to at least 150 times its present size, filling the sky. Finally, the outer layers will blow off, leaving just a burned-out core.

Below *As the sun expands, the earth will begin to dry out and huge dust storms will occur, making much of the planet's surface unsuitable for growing food.*

Left The barren landscapes of Mars, as pictured here by Pathfinder in 1997, suggest what the earth will look like in five billion years' time.

NEW WORLDS

For the human race to survive the death of the sun, people will have to leave our solar system (the collection of planets and moons that orbit our Sun) and find a planet orbiting a younger star in a different solar system. This incredible journey will probably take place in stages, as we start colonies on ever-more distant planets.

Below *Although it is impossible to truly imagine how the earth will look when the sun eventually expands, the devastation caused by a widespread forest fire gives some idea.*

FAST GETAWAY?

While the earth is roasted by the massively expanding Sun, huge spaceships called space arks will transport people, animals, and plants to another planet orbiting a younger star. By this time, though, we will probably have colonized many new worlds — so that no single disaster like the sun's death will threaten the human race.

DEATH OF OUR SUN

ADVANCE WARNING?	🟢	🟢	🟢	🟢	🟢
SCIENCE IS SOUND	🟢	🟢	🟢	🟢	🟢
ESCAPABLE?	🟢	🟢	🟢	🟠	🟠
HOW SOON?	🟢	🟢	🟢	🟢	🟢

BRAVE NEW WORLDS

The conclusion to life on this planet need not mean the end of the human race. Future generations will begin to look at ways of escaping from the earth before the planet dies.

A NEW STAR
One possible means of escape was first proposed by the science-fiction writer Arthur C. Clarke in his book *2010: Odyssey Two* (1982). The massive planet Jupiter is really a failed star. If we could somehow add more mass to it, it might explode into life and become a new Sun. There are several moons orbiting the planet, four of which might be adapted to suit human life. In this way, we could create an entirely new solar system arranged around Jupiter.

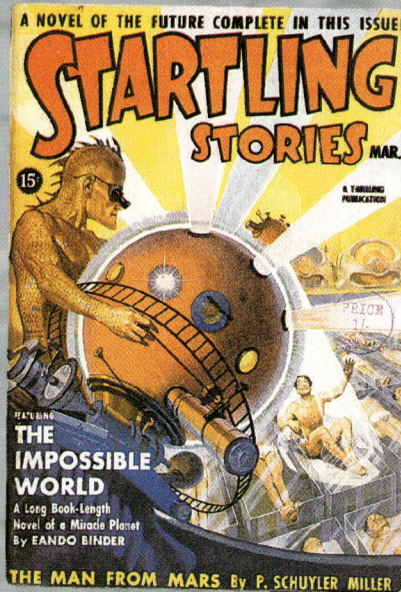

A NOVEL OF THE FUTURE COMPLETE IN THIS ISSUE!

STARTLING STORIES MAR.

15¢

THE IMPOSSIBLE WORLD
A Long Book-Length Novel of a Miracle Planet
By EANDO BINDER

THE MAN FROM MARS by P. SCHUYLER MILLER

Left *In the event of a global disaster in the future, people may be forced to start again on another planet such as Mars, as suggested by this science-fiction magazine cover.*

SLEEPING PASSENGERS
Another way we could escape our fate is in huge space arks. (*see* page 27). Since these arks would travel for thousands of years across space, people aboard would spend the whole journey in "cryogenic suspension" — a form of deep sleep, which is now in its early development stages.

One day our descendants may look back across space and point to the remains of a once-blue planet orbiting a fading star and say "That is where all human life began."

Left *Between now and the death of the sun after five billion years, it is possible that we will be visited by at least one alien species. If they have the technology to reach us from their planet, then they may understand the problems facing the earth in the future. They might even invite some people to escape to their world with them, ensuring the human race would continue to exist after our Sun has burned itself out.*

JUPITER MISSIONS

Jupiter and its moons are being studied in more detail now than ever before. The Galileo spacecraft has been sending back pictures and data since 1995. Jupiter's moons could become the destination for peopled spacecraft in the coming centuries.

ESCAPE FROM EARTH

FEASIBLE TECHNOLOGY	●	●	●	●	●
SCIENCE IS SOUND	●	●	●	●	●
AFFORDABLE	●	●	●	●	●
HOW SOON?	●	●	●	●	●

GLOSSARY

ANTIBIOTIC
A drug used to fight microorganisms that cause diseases.

ASTEROID
A relatively small object in orbit around the sun made of rock and iron. They are usually found in a belt between the orbits of Mars and Jupiter. The largest asteroid, Ceres, is 620 miles in diameter. Asteroids are believed to be fragments left over after the formation of the solar system.

BACTERIA
Simple, single-celled organisms. They are among the smallest living things. There are thousands of types of bacteria, most of which are harmless to living things. Some species are harmful and can cause diseases in humans.

BLACK HOLE
A mysterious object possessing a gravity so great that nothing, not even light, can escape from it. At the center of a black hole is an area of infinite density where matter is all but crushed out of existence. So far, four black holes have been detected in our galaxy.

CELL
The smallest unit of living matter that is able to maintain an independent existence. When grouped together, cells form tissues, such as muscle. In the human body, different cells have different functions.

COMET
A relatively small object composed of ice and dust traveling in a very long orbit around the sun. As the comet approaches the sun, a trail of gas and dust is thrown off, forming the familiar "tail."

CONSTELLATION
One of 88 areas in the sky divided by astronomers in 1930 to make identification and classification easier.

DENSE
An object that is tightly packed. Dense objects have a large mass — they contain a large amount of matter, making them heavy — but are relatively small in size.

EVOLUTION
The process by which species change from one form to another and develop specialized characteristics over long periods of time. These characteristics help them to adapt to their environment. Evolution has produced the billions of different species that live on the earth today.

GALAXY
A collection of millions, or even billions, of stars held together by their mutual gravity. Our Sun belongs to a spiral-shaped galaxy that is called the Milky Way.

GAS
A form of matter in which molecules are loosely connected, and behave in a random manner. Air is an example of gas.

GENE
The chemical instructions, at the heart of cells, that determine how living things live and develop.

GRAVITY
A force that attracts an object possessing mass (an amount of matter, which gives it weight) to any other object possessing mass. It can be likened to magnetic attraction.

LIGHT-YEAR

The distance that light travels through space in one Earth year. As light travels at 186,420 miles per second under these conditions, one light-year is equal to a distance of 5.8 trillion miles.

METEOR

An asteroid that enters the earth's atmosphere from space and burns up before reaching the surface of our planet.

METEORITE

An asteroid from space that survives the journey through the earth's atmosphere and crashes into the surface of the planet.

MOLECULE

A group of at least two atoms, which are bonded together.

NEUTRON STAR

A small, dense star composed mostly of tiny particles called neutrons. They tend to be no more than 12 miles in diameter. If they were much bigger, they would become black holes.

ORBIT

The path taken through space by one body (such as the earth) around another (such as the sun).

PLANET

A large body, such as the earth, which is in orbit around a star (in our case, the sun). Planets are composed of rock, metal, or gas, or a combination of the three.

RADIO TELESCOPE

A device for detecting radio waves arriving at the earth from other parts of the universe. In essence, a radio telescope is a large radio receiver.

SATELLITE

Objects that orbit a planet. They can be natural, such as moons, or artificial, such as communication satellites.

SOLAR SYSTEM

A star and all the bodies that are in orbit around it. Our solar system is made up of the sun, the planets Mercury, Venus, Earth, Mars, Jupiter, Saturn, Uranus, Neptune, and Pluto, along with many moons, asteroids, and comets.

STAR

A huge sphere, composed mostly of hydrogen and helium, which produces light and heat as a result of nuclear reactions at its core. In order for these reactions to occur, the star must possess a mass at least 80 times that of the planet Jupiter. The sun is an example of a star.

SUPERNOVA

The explosion of a massive star. When a supernova occurs, the star temporarily becomes about 100 times brighter than our Sun. They occur, on average, about once every 100 years in our galaxy.

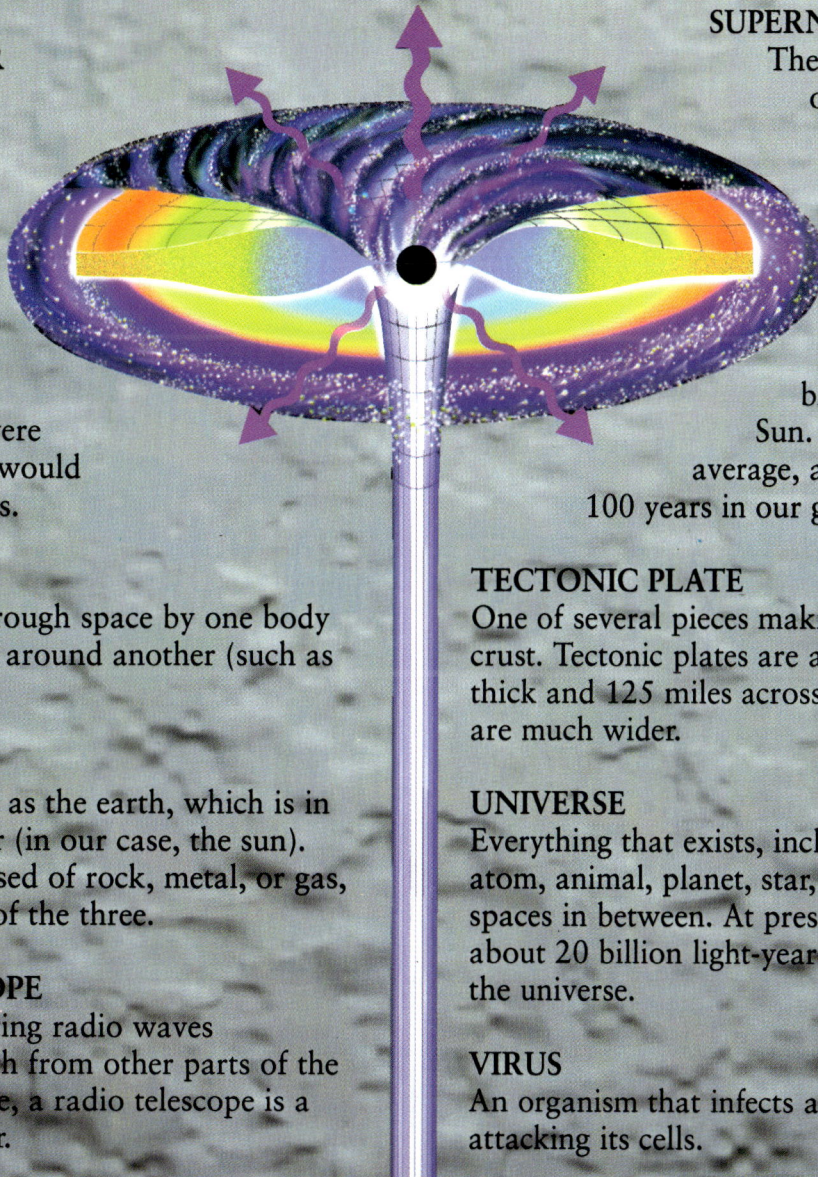

TECTONIC PLATE

One of several pieces making up the earth's crust. Tectonic plates are about 60 miles thick and 125 miles across, although some are much wider.

UNIVERSE

Everything that exists, including every atom, animal, planet, star, galaxy, and the spaces in between. At present, it would take about 20 billion light-years to travel across the universe.

VIRUS

An organism that infects a body by attacking its cells.

INDEX